TABLE OF CONTENTS

CHANGE IS ALL AROUND US

How we live changes the places we live.

Where we live changes us too.

LET'S EXPLORE

People have always searched for new and different places.

Long ago, people explored to settle new lands and trade goods.

OFF THEY GO

Europeans **colonized** many places in the 1400s. In most of these places, there were already people living there, and the colonists usually treated them poorly.

Settlers' lives changed.
They lived in a new land.

They ate new foods.
They wore new clothes.

ON THE MOVE

People move from one place to another. This is called **migration**.

We bring our **culture** with us when we move.

Sometimes many cultures come together.

We bring great ideas with us too. Sharing them can change the world.

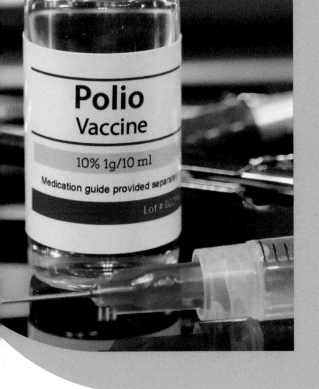

DID YOU KNOW?

The "Brown Box" was the first video game console ever! The inventor moved from Germany to the United States.

NATURE CALLS

How we live changes nature.
Our decisions affect our
furry friends.

People produce **pollution**. This hurts our health and our planet.

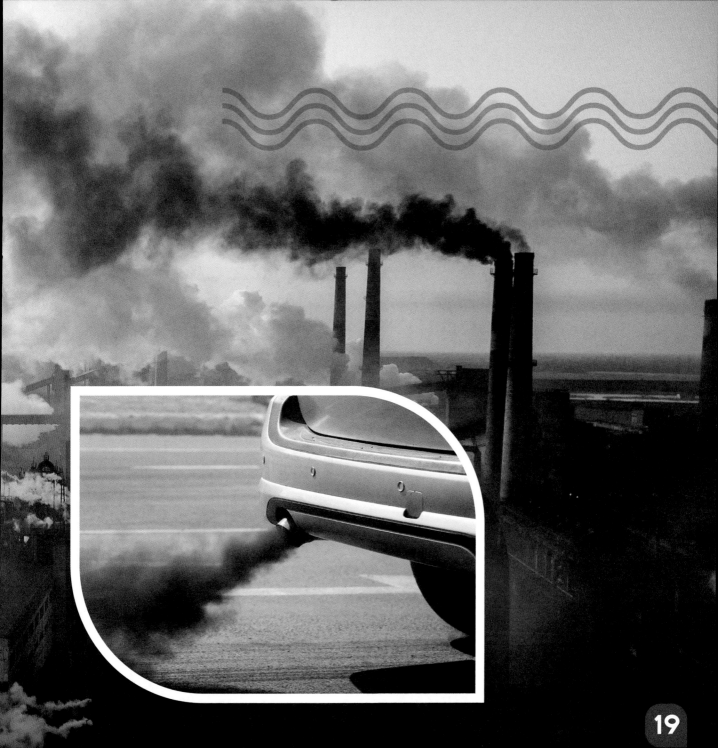

But people can also do things to protect our planet.

This makes the world a better place for all of us!

PLANT A TREE

Trees clean our air, provide homes for animals, prevent soil erosion, and more!

PHOTO GLOSSARY

colonized (KAH-luh-nized): established a new colony in a place

culture (KUHL-chur): the art, ideas, customs, traditions, and ways of life of a group of people

migration (mye-GRAY-shuhn): movement of people from one region to another

pollution (puh-LOO-shuhn): harmful materials that damage or contaminate the air, water, and soil

MAKE A PLASTIC BOTTLE PLANTER

Supplies

scissors

seeds

plastic soda bottle

water

dirt

Directions

1. With an adult, cut the top half off of the plastic bottle. Set it aside.
2. With an adult, poke a few small holes in the bottom of the bottom half (for drainage).
3. Fill the bottom half with dirt.
4. In the dirt, plant seeds. These can be flowers, fruits, or veggies. You can also plant dried beans or peas from your kitchen.
5. Water them lightly. Set the top half back on it. This will hold in moisture.
6. Set your planter in a sunny spot. Watch your seedlings grow!

How long did it take for your seeds to sprout? Once they have sprouted, what do you think you should do with them?

INDEX

ABOUT THE AUTHOR

Shantel Gobin is an educator and global citizen. She enjoys living in Brooklyn, New York. She is a life-long learner who loves exploring. It is her goal to make the world a better place.

AFTER-READING ACTIVITY

With a parent, go online and do some research. Explore inventions made by people who immigrated to your country. Discuss your research with a family member.

Library of Congress PCN Data

We Change Places, Places Change Us / Shantel Gobin
(Social Studies Connect)
ISBN 978-1-73165-633-9 (hard cover)(alk. paper)
ISBN 978-1-73165-606-3 (soft cover)
ISBN 978-1-73165-615-5 (eBook)
ISBN 978-1-73165-624-7 (ePub)
Library of Congress Control Number: 2022943190

Rourke Educational Media
Printed in the United States of America
01-0372311937

© 2023 Rourke Educational Media

www.rourkebooks.com

Edited by: Catherine Malaski
Cover design by: Morgan Burnside
Interior design by: Morgan Burnside
Photo Credits: Cover, page 1: ©Jacob Lund/ Shutterstock.com, ©Rawpixel.com/ Shutterstock.com; Cover, pages 1, 4: ©Zurijeta/ Shutterstock.com; Cover, pages 1, 20: ©Rawpixel.com/ Shutterstock.com; pages 4-5: ©Liu zishan/ Shutterstock.com; pages 6-7: ©Pavel Mozharov/ Shutterstock.com; page 7: ©Dmitrijs Kaminskis/ Shutterstock.com; page 8: ©Everett Collection/ Shutterstock.com; page 9: ©Library of Congress, Prints and Photographs Division, John C.H. Grabill Collection, [reproduction number, e.g., LC-USZ62-90145]; pages 10-11: ©Andrey_Popov/ Shutterstock.com; page 11: ©Wayne Hutchinson/Newscom; page 12: ©Dina Julayeva/ Shutterstock.com; page 13: ©Gorodenkoff/ Shutterstock.com; page 14: ©licensed under the Creative Commons Attribution 4.0 International license; page 15: ©Bernard Chantal/ Shutterstock.com, ©Division of Medicine and Science, National Museum of American History, Smithsonian Institution; pages 16-17: ©CherylRamalho/ Shutterstock.com; page 17: ©Eric Buermeyer/ Shutterstock.com, ESB Professional/ Shutterstock.com; pages 18-19: ©TR STOK/ Shutterstock.com; page 19: ©Toa55/ Shutterstock.com; pages 19-20: ©Rawpixel.com/ Shutterstock.com; page 21: ©Rawpixel.com/ Shutterstock.com; page 22: ©sci Media/ Shutterstock.com, ©Rido/ Shutterstock.com, Janossy Gergely/ Shutterstock.com, Romolo Tavani/ Shutterstock.com.